The promise
The story of Abraham and Isaac

The story so far

JON couldn't get on with his homework. He had to write a love story, and it had to come from the Bible. "Love stories are for wimps," he moaned.

His computer mouse whisked him through the computer screen into a book-filled study. There he met the Scribe.

"I'll show you a love story," said the Scribe.

The Scribe took him back to the time when God made Adam and Eve and a fabulous garden. An evil angel called Satan turned them against God. They were thrown out of the garden, but the damage had been done. A virus had come into the Earth.

Adam and Eve had two sons. In an ice-cold rage, the elder son killed his brother. The virus was at work. Years passed and the evil spread. Everyone except Noah and his family died in a massive flood. More years passed and again people messed everything up.

all worship the moon. But somehow he can't bring himself to pray to the moon. He's certain there's a real God who made the moon. He prays to this God.

"And God loves Abraham. Don't forget I promised you a love story."

 "Who's that bloke over there? He looks kinda lonely."

"That's Abraham. He's step one in God's master plan to save the world."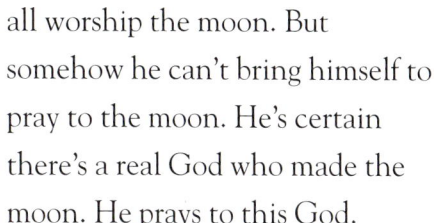

 "What can one man do?"

"It's a beginning. Now what did I tell you?"

 "I know. Shema – listen."

"Where was I? Oh yes, you're right about one thing. Abraham is rather lonely. He's out of step with everyone in his town. They

"A bit of a wash out so far, what with the flood an' all."

"God doesn't give up. One day he speaks to Abraham."

"God says, 'Abraham. I want you to leave this town, and your house and your relatives. You're to move to a new land. I'm going to make you famous. People all over the world will be happy, because of you.'

"It's quite a shock, I can tell you. Abraham is 75 years old."

"That's older than my Gran. Where are they off to?"

"That's the strange thing. God doesn't say. Abraham has to learn to trust him."

"Abraham doesn't argue. He packs up and sets off, with his wife Sarah, who's 65, by the way, and Lot, who's his nephew. Abraham and Sarah don't have any children of their own.

"They take all their possessions loaded on to camels and donkeys. And their servants go along, too. It's quite an adventure. Everyone thinks they're mad.

"They sleep in tents."

"Great! Count me in. I went camping last summer."

"They travel hundreds of miles. They go south through the

hills and mountains of Canaan. One day Abraham camps near a great old oak tree. And God speaks to him again.

"God says: 'Look around you to the north and south and east and west. I'm giving all this land to you and your family.'

"And Abraham believes God's promise.

 "Later God speaks again to Abraham. He says, 'Look at the sky and count the stars if you can. This will be the number of your descendants.'"

"Wow! That's a lot of descendants. Does descendants mean children, and their children and their children, Mr Scribe?"

"Yes – but have you spotted the snag?"

"Er . . . didn't you say Abraham and Sarah had no children?"

"Right. And what's more, they're very old. All the same, Abraham believes God's promise.

"When Abraham is 99 years old and Sarah is 89 years old God speaks to him again. 'I am God all powerful,' he says. 'Next year Sarah will have a baby boy. Nothing is impossible for me to do.'"

 "You've got to be joking."

"That's what Sarah thinks. She says, 'A baby? What rubbish! I'm too old.' And she laughs."

 "What happened?"

"Come and see."

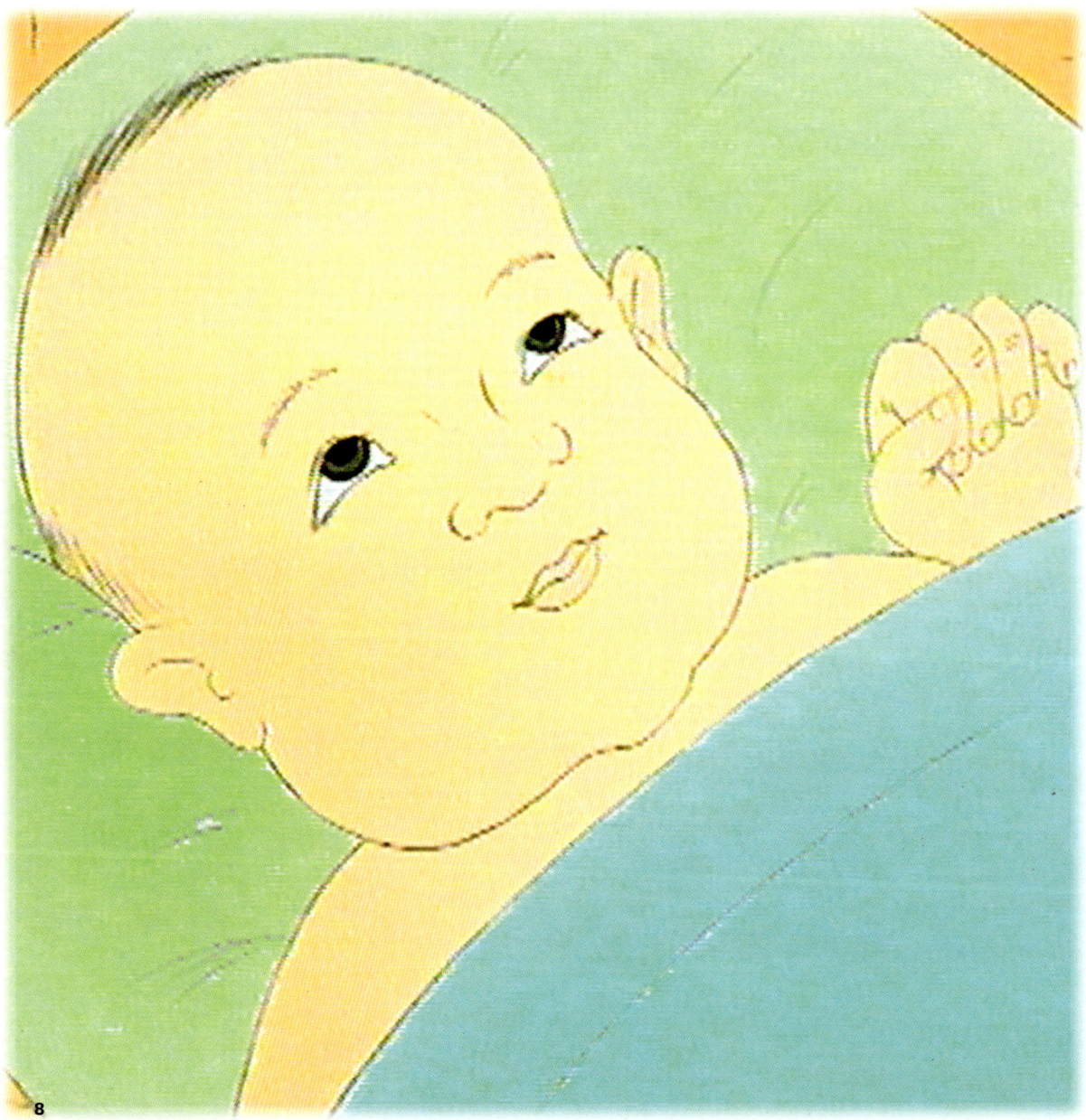

'Now Sarah is really laughing. They call their son 'Isaac', which means, 'he laughs'. They're devoted to him."

 "My parents are devoted to my kid sister."

 "Do you have tests at school?"

"Yuk. What's that got to do with anything?"

"Why do your teachers give you tests?"

"To make us learn, I s'pose."

"Soon Abraham is going to have the biggest test of his life. A nightmare of a test."

"One day God says to Abraham, 'Take your son Isaac, who you love, and go to the land of Moriah. I will show you a mountain there. Climb the mountain, and at the top build an altar.'"

"What's an altar?"

"It's a small pile of stones and earth with a flat top. It used to be where animals were killed and burnt, as a sacrifice to God. Now that Jesus Christ has come, nobody does this any more. There's no need. But that's another story."

"Go on."

"God said, 'Kill your son Isaac, and burn him on the altar as a sacrifice to me.'"

"Eeeeeeeek."

"That's weird. It's cruel. And what about the promise?"

"Abraham has learnt to trust God. He's not worried."

"I would be, especially if I were Isaac."

"Isaac doesn't know – yet."

"Early the next morning Abraham gets up and saddles the donkey. He cuts wood for the sacrifice, slides a dagger in his belt, and puts a small fire in a container.

"He sets out, with Isaac and two servants."

 "Where're the servants and the donkey?"

 "Abraham has told the servants to wait for him at the foot of the mountain. Now Isaac has a problem."

"You can say that again."

 "He says to his dad, 'We've got the fire and the wood, but where's the lamb for the sacrifice?'

"Abraham says, 'God will provide the lamb for the sacrifice.'"

"Oh no! I don't want to see this! Can't you stop him?"

"Don't be scared. Listen.
"Abraham is just pulling out his dagger when God calls to him."

"God says, 'Don't kill your son, or hurt him in any way. Now it is clear that you really love me, as I love you. You were ready to give up your only son for me, as I would for you. But look! I have provided the offering for you.

"'Take this sheep and kill it on the altar.'"

"Phew!"

"Abraham gave that place a name. He called it: 'The Lord will provide'."

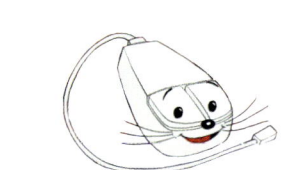

"Abraham believed God and trusted him. And God didn't let Abraham down. He kept his promise. Isaac grew up and had children and his children had children. And on and on.

"That land of Canaan which God promised to Abraham's family is called Israel today. And all the Jews and all the Arabs in the world think of Abraham as their very first ancestor.

"And all Christians think of Abraham as their father as well. Everybody who trusts God and believes what he says is like Abraham.

"But remember that vicious serpent way back in the Garden? And remember the virus that infected Planet Earth? They didn't go away. The rest of the story has a lot of nasty moments. But through it all, God never stops loving the people – as you'll see if you listen on."

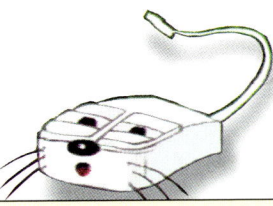

You can read the whole story of Abraham in the Bible, in the book of Genesis, from chapters 12 to 25. You can read these stories from the life of Abraham in Genesis chapters 12, 18, 21 and 22.